POISONED LAN

D0825392

BOOKS BY JOHN MONTAGUE

poetry
A Chosen Light
Tides
The Rough Field
A Slow Dance

*

short stories
Death of a Chieftain

*

editor: The Faber Book of Irish Verse

JOHN MONTAGUE

Poisoned Lands

Oui, l'ouragan allait bientôt venir;
Mais cela valait-il la peine que l'on en parlât et
  qu'on dérangeât l'avenir?
Là où nous sommes, il n'y a pas de crainte urgente.

RENÉ CHAR, *Les Inventeurs*

THE DOLMEN PRESS
LONDON : OXFORD UNIVERSITY PRESS

Set in Times Roman type and printed and published
in the Republic of Ireland at the Dolmen Press,
North Richmond Industrial Estate, North Richmond Street, Dublin 1

ISBN 0 85105 319 X THE DOLMEN PRESS
ISBN 0 19 211869 2 OXFORD UNIVERSITY PRESS

First published by MacGibbon and Kee Limited, 1961

New edition 1977
in association with Oxford University Press

Oxford University Press, Walton Street, Oxford OX2 6DP
OXFORD LONDON GLASGOW NEW YORK
TORONTO MELBOURNE WELLINGTON CAPE TOWN
IBADAN NAIROBI DAR ES SALAAM LUSAKA ADDIS ABABA
KUALA LUMPUR SINGAPORE JAKARTA HONG KONG TOKYO
DELHI BOMBAY CALCUTTA MADRAS KARACHI

Distributed in the U.S.A. and in Canada by
Humanities Press Inc., 171 First Avenue, Atlantic Highlands, N.J. 07716

*

We acknowledge the assistance of The Arts Council of Northern Ireland
in the production of this book

for Roger McHugh

Some who travel light
May feel deprived
Of all the love that weighs
On other people's lives.

CONTENTS

INTRODUCTION

Revising these poems has been a strange experience, the reverse almost of Henry James's late story, 'The Jolly Corner.' It became not so much the case of an older writer wishing to correct his younger self as of trying to release that earlier self from chains of time and place.

A marooned Northerner, I began to write as a student in post-war — sorry, Emergency — Dublin. A third of the poems in the book date from the early Fifties when I was discovering with awe that I might possibly be able to write something like the kind of modern poetry I admired. But the literary atmosphere was against it, and while I found lonely allies in people like Valentin Iremonger, what prevailed in the poetic world of Dublin was acrimony and insult; a poem was to be kicked, not examined; the begrudgers ruled. I admired Patrick Kavanagh but his baffled fury was that of a man flailing between two faded worlds, the country he had left, and the literary Dublin he never found.

Such an ingrown, discouraging climate meant that my leaving for America became partly a flight. I recovered slowly there, and met writers of my own age, whether Snodgrass and Bly in the Middle West, or Snyder and Ginsberg in California, for whom poetry was a craft and a vision. On the wing, and wounded, I wrote little, but by 1956 I felt strong enough to return to Ireland; was indeed, helped to, by the generous friend to whom this book is dedicated, who found me, that most useful of things, a decent job.

So the second group of poems begin in the late Fifties when I had revived the dialogue with my earlier self. The atmosphere was more cordial, thanks also to the Dolmen Press, which produced *Forms of Exile* in late 1958. My taste was becoming surer and I remember receiving a letter from Robert Graves, one of my heroes, altering a word in 'The First Invasion of Ireland' (I leave you to guess which) with a charming apology: 'few poems are worth a comment nowadays.' But when I came to gather *Poisoned Lands* (1961) I still suppressed poems in a way that now seems part of the malaise of the period, an unconscious censorship, a fear of emotion, of deliberate Irishism, of ruralism. How could we anticipate that the harshness of factory farming would revive the bucolic dream?

After sixteen years, a few changes are inevitable. If the rhetoric of 'Rome, Anno Santo' refused to be shaped into shorter stanzas, 'The Water Carrier' regained a lost stanza. An archaeological anachronism had to be removed from 'The Sean Bhean Bhocht' and the Eluard awaits a future anthology of recent French poetry. Altogether, this new edition of *Poisoned Lands* is much closer to what it should have been and if I drop a few poems I can no longer stomach, I include several that I then smothered. I notice the reticence where love is concerned but plead that I have tried to make up for it since. As for the oppressive note that glooms through the whole collection, may it not have been prophetic?

A final period vignette. An editor-poet I studiously avoided was T. S. Eliot but when the volume was being considered for American publication, it crossed his desk. Old Possum risked a friendly pat: 'I have, indeed, found Mr. Montague's poems worthy of study.' I hope they still are; and that they give pleasure as well.

JOHN MONTAGUE
Cork 1976

THE WATER CARRIER

Twice daily I carried water from the spring,
Morning before leaving for school, and evening;
Balanced as a fulcrum between two buckets.

A bramble rough path ran to the river
Where one stepped carefully across slime-topped stones,
With corners abraded as bleakly white as bones.

At the widening pool (for washing and cattle)
Minute fish flickered as one dipped,
Circling to fill, with rust-tinged water.

The second or enamel bucket was for spring water
Which, after racing through a rushy meadow,
Came bubbling in a broken drain-pipe,

Corroded wafer thin with rust.
It ran so pure and cold, it fell
Like manacles of ice on the wrists.

One stood until the bucket brimmed
Inhaling the musty smell of unpicked berries,
That heavy greenness fostered by water.

Recovering the scene, I had hoped to stylize it,
Like the portrait of an Egyptian water-carrier:
Yet halt, entranced by slight but memoried life.

I sometimes come to take the water there,
Not as return or refuge, but some pure thing,
Some living source, half-imagined and half-real

Pulses in the fictive water that I feel.

THE SEAN BHEAN BHOCHT

As a child I was frightened by her
Busy with her bowl of tea in a farmhouse chimney corner,
Wrapped in a cocoon of rags and shawls.
The Lord have mercy on him,
'Go ndeanaidh Dia trocaire ar a anam.'
She rocked and crooned,
A doll's head mouthing under stained rafters.

'The fairies of Ireland and the fairies of Scotland
'Fought on that hill all night
'And in the morning the well ran blood.
'The dead queen was buried on that hill.
'St. Patrick passed by the cross:
'There is the mark of a footprint forever
'Where he stood to pray.'

Eyes rheumy with racial memory;
Fragments of bread soaked in brown tea
And eased between shrunken gums.
Her clothes stank like summer flax;
Watched all day as she swayed
Towards death between memories and prayers
By a farmer's child in a rough play-box.

'Mrs. McGurren had the evil eye,
'She prayed prayers on the black cow:
'It dropped there and died,
'Dropped dead in its tracks.
'She stood on the mearing and cursed the Clarkes:
'They never had a good day since,
'Fluke and bad crops and a child born strange.'

In the groove a running-down record,
Heavy with local history:
Only the scratching now, the labouring breath,
Prophecy rattling aged bones.
Age is neither knowledge nor authority,
Though it may claim both,
Weaving a litany of legends against death.

But in high summer as the hills burned with corn
I strode through golden light
To the secret spirals of the burial stone:
The grass-choked well ran sluggish red —
Not with blood but ferrous rust —
But beneath the whorls of the guardian stone
What hidden queen lay dust?

1957

LIKE DOLMENS ROUND MY CHILDHOOD, THE OLD PEOPLE

Like dolmens round my childhood, the old people.

Jamie MacCrystal sang to himself,
A broken song without tune, without words;
He tipped me a penny every pension day,
Fed kindly crusts to winter birds.
When he died, his cottage was robbed,
Mattress and money box torn and searched.
Only the corpse they didn't disturb.

Maggie Owens was surrounded by animals,
A mongrel bitch and shivering pups,
Even in her bedroom a she-goat cried.
She was a well of gossip defiled,
Fanged chronicler of a whole countryside;
Reputed a witch, all I could find
Was her lonely need to deride.

The Nialls lived along a mountain lane
Where heather bells bloomed, clumps of foxglove.
All were blind, with Blind Pension and Wireless,
Dead eyes serpent-flicked as one entered
To shelter from a downpour of mountain rain.
Crickets chirped under the rocking hearthstone
Until the muddy sun shone out again.

Mary Moore lived in a crumbling gatehouse,
Famous as Pisa for its leaning gable.
Bag-apron and boots, she tramped the fields
Driving lean cattle from a miry stable.
A by-word for fierceness, she fell asleep
Over love stories, Red Star and Red Circle,
Dreamed of gypsy love rites, by firelight sealed.

Wild Billy Eagleson married a Catholic servant girl
When all his Loyal family passed on:
We danced round him shouting 'To Hell with King Billy',
And dodged from the arc of his flailing blackthorn.
Forsaken by both creeds, he showed little concern
Until the Orange drums banged past in the summer
And bowler and sash aggressively shone.

Curate and doctor trudged to attend them,
Through knee-deep snow, through summer heat,
From main road to lane to broken path,
Gulping the mountain air with painful breath.
Sometimes they were found by neighbours,
Silent keepers of a smokeless hearth,
Suddenly cast in the mould of death.

Ancient Ireland, indeed! I was reared by her bedside,
The rune and the chant, evil eye and averted head,
Fomorian fierceness of family and local feud.
Gaunt figures of fear and of friendliness,
For years they trespassed on my dreams,
Until once, in a standing circle of stones,
I felt their shadows pass

Into that dark permanence of ancient forms.

SICK CALL
for Séamus

When the doctor disappeared
Under the thatched lintel
To tend a farmer who had
Fallen under his tractor
I tramped moodily back
And forwards in the snow

Meeting my own drowning
Footprints, as I turned,
Seeing, as the dog barked,
The trees, isolated and black
Against the grey, whirling
Bowl of the sky.

From the oblong of light
His wife called me over,
To relate, confidentially,
(The cur whining at her apron)
How hard it was, having
Her husband 'in a bad way'.

As my brother's car rocked
Down the rutted lane
Scattering a powder of snow,
The dog resumed its yelping,
Plunging at the wheels
And back to safety again.

A DRINK OF MILK

In the girdered dark
of the byre, cattle move;
warm engines hushed
to a siding groove

before the switch flicks
down for milking.
In concrete partitions
they rattle their chains

while the farmhand eases
rubber tentacles to tug
lightly but rhythmically
on their swollen dugs

and up the pale cylinders
of the milking machine
mounts an untouched
steadily pulsing stream.

Only the tabby steals
to dip its radar whiskers
with old fashioned relish
in a chipped saucer

and before Seán lurches
to kick his boots off
in the night-silent kitchen
he draws a mug of froth

to settle on the sideboard
under the hoard of delph.
A pounding transistor shakes
the Virgin on her shelf

as he dreams towards bed.
A last glance at a magazine,
he puts the mug to his head,
grunts, and drains it clean.

MURPHY IN MANCHESTER

He wakes to a confused dream of boats, gulls,
And all his raw present floats
Suddenly up to him on rocking rails.
Through that long first day
He trudges streets, tracks friends,
Stares open-mouthed at monuments
To manufacturers, sabred generals.
Passing a vegetable stall
With exposed fruits, he halts
To contemplate a knobbly vegetable.

At lunchtime, in a cafeteria,
He finds his feet and hands
Enlarge, become like foreign lands.
A great city is darkness, noise
Through which bright girls move
Like burnished other children's toys.
Soon the whistling factory
Will lock him in:
Half-stirred memories and regrets
Drawn into that iron din.

MIDLAND VILLAGE

Down by the ballalley the men are congregated.
A handball cracks against concrete or loops
Across the safety net, a sudden parabola.

Spectators lounge, dark as fish in pools.
Only a shadowy girl, cycling slowly,
Starts disturbance among the shoals.

Bats whir in and out of an old stable
Where children play at war with wooden guns
And a Duffy's Circus poster flakes from the walls.

Crows brawl in the ivy of the old abbey
As over the flat, weed-choked fields
A donkey raises its rusty commentary,

*

To taunt an exile in some industrial town
For years, with an image of unchanging life;
To torment the respectable one who stays

With too much stillness, till, mouth ablaze
With tosspit oaths, he parades starkly down
The street, madness severing his last link

With this soft world — a gelding knife.

A ROYAL VISIT

Tara, though she be desolate to-day,
Once was the habitation of heroes . . .

from *The Book of Leinster*

I

The deep cooing of doves
As we move towards the earthen fort
Is a subtly insidious music
Designed to exhort:
Axehead of the intellect washed
In hovering fragrance of hawthorn,
The primary colours of a summer morning.

II

This martial extravagance of mounds
Cannot be approached simply:
Through ritual sagas it resounds
With din of war and love.
Devious virgins and fisty men
Gesturing against the sky,
Invoke the seasonal crucifixion.

III

Gaelic Acropolis or smoky hovel?
In the enormous osiered banquet hall,
The sotted bards rehearse
A genealogical glory:
Stately assonance of verse
Petrifies wolf-skinned warriors
In galleries of race.

IV

Who longs for subtler singing,
Muted vocal of the dove,
Seeks erotic terror ringing
Over stony beds of love:
Couple and landscape blended,
Till beneath the hunchback mountain
Plunges the boar of death.

V

A battle of miracles
Proves the Christian dispensation,
Druidic snow turning
To merciful Christian rain:
Christ is the greater magician.
No more the phallic stone
Screams for its ritual king.

VI

A mournful St. Patrick surveys
This provincial magnificence;
He sees what twitching sentries saw
When five regal roads
Across a landscape drew:
The central lands of Meath dissolve
Into royal planes of blue.

OLD MYTHOLOGIES

And now, at last, all proud deeds done,
Mouths dust-stopped, dark they embrace
Suitably disposed, as urns, underground.
Cattle munching soft spring grass
— Epicures of shamrock and the four-leaved clover —
Hear a whimper of ancient weapons,
As a whole dormitory of heroes turn over,
Regretting their butchers' days.
This valley cradles their archaic madness
As once, on an impossibly epic morning,
It upheld their savage stride:
To bagpiped battle marching,
Wolfhounds, lean as models,
At their urgent heels.

ANNO SANTO

I

Under the colonnades of St. Peter's crescent
The spray of the fountain lisps against the sun.
Ranked façades proclaim a church's humanism,
Bernini's baroque flares out in stately ecstasy
But the Irish matrons, girded in nun-like black,
Pilgrims from Georgian buildings above the slow canal,
Or stone-fenced fields beside the Atlantic's wrack
March towards their God, with bead and book, relentlessly.

II

Being tired, sleeping, wisdom is smuggled in
In many strange ways; as in an Italian town
Where dogs barked and people stared
I drank cold water and stretched asleep on stone:
So does wisdom form,
Simple as sweat on skin,
As water on the palate, cooling, thin.

A FOOTNOTE ON MONASTICISM:
DINGLE PENINSULA

In certain places, still, surprisingly, you come
Upon them, resting like old straw hats set down
Beside the sea, weather-beaten but enduring
For a dozen centuries: here the mound
That was the roof has slithered in
And the outlines you can barely trace:
Nor does it matter since every wilderness
Along this rocky coast retains more signs
In ragged groupings of these cells and caves,
Of where the hermits, fiercely dispossessed,
Found refuge among gulls and rocks
The incessant prayer of nearby waves.

Among darkening rocks he prayed,
Body chastened and absurd,
An earth-bound dragging space
His spirit blundered like a bird:
Hands, specialised by prayer,
Like uplifted chalices,
Nightly proferring the self
To soundless, perfect messengers.

There are times, certainly, looking through a window
At amiable clustered humanity, or scanning
The leaves of some old book, that one might wish
To join their number, start a new and fashionable
Sect beside the Celtic sea, long favourable
To dreams and dreamers; anchorites whose love
Was selfishly alone, a matter so great
That only to stone could they whisper it:
Breaking the obstinate structure of flesh
With routine of vigil and fast,
Till water-cress stirred on the palate
Like the movement of a ghost.

In ceaseless labour of the spirit,
Isolate, unblessed;
Until quietude of the senses
Announces presence of a guest;
Desolation final,
Rock within and rock without
Till from the stubborn rock of the heart
The purifying waters spurt.

1953

SOLILOQUY ON A SOUTHERN STRAND

A priest, holidaying on the coast outside Sydney, thinks nostalgically of his boyhood in Ireland.

When I was young, it was much simpler;
I saw God standing on a local hill,
His eyes were gentle and soft birds
Sang in chorus to his voice until
My body trembled, ardent in submission.
The friar came to preach the yearly sermon
For Retreat, and cried among the flaring candles:
'O children, children, if you but knew,
'Each hair is counted, everything you do
'Offends or sweetens His five wounds!'
A priest with a harsh and tuneless voice,
Raising his brown-robed arms to cry:
'Like this candle-end, the body gutters out to die!'
Calling us all to do penance and rejoice.

Hearing the preacher speak, I knew my mind
And wished to serve, leaving the friendly farm
For years of college. At first I found it strange
And feared the boys with smoother hands and voices:
I lay awake at night, longed for home.
I heard the town boys laughing in the dark
At things that made me burn with shame,
And where the votive candles whispered into wax
Hesitantly I spoke my treasured doubts,
Conquering all my passions in your Name.
I weathered years of sameness
Until I stood before the Cathedral altar,
A burly country boy but new-made priest;
My mother watched in happiness and peace.

The young people crowd the shore now,
Rushing from Sydney, like lemmings, to the sea.
Heat plays upon the glaring cluttered beach,
Casts as in a mould my beaten head and knees.
New cars come swooping in like birds
To churn and chop the dust. A wireless,
Stuck in the sand, crackles static
As girls are roughed and raced
With whirling beach-balls in the sun.
What here avails my separate cloth,
My sober self, whose meaning contradicts
The sensual drama they enact in play?
'Hot Lips, Hot Lips', the throaty singer sighs:
A young man preens aloft and dives.

Is this the proper ending for a man?
The Pacific waves crash in upon the beach,
Roll and rise and inward stretch upon the beach.
It is December now and warm,
And yet my blood is cold, my shoulders slack;
In slow submission, I turn my body
Up to the sun, as on a rack,
Enduring comfort. In a dream,
I hear the cuckoo dance his double notes,
Among the harvest stooks like golden chessmen;
Each call, an age, a continent between.
No martyrdom, no wonder, no patent loss:
Is it for this mild ending that I
Have carried, all this way, my cross?

California, 1956

DIRGE OF THE MAD PRIEST

God watches from the cracked mirror on the wall.
God is a peeping-Tom, cat-like watches all.
When the stallion plunges, God is the rider,
With dark beard, back straight as a wall.
When I cut my hand or cheek in shaving
His blood flows and there is nothing at all
To protect me from the shadow of his redemption,
My godhead hung in text of terror on the wall.

As I pass in the street the young girls cry,
Lift their light skirts and cry,
And the blackbird mocks from the cherry-tree,
Lifting its wings to cry:
'Shapeless, shapeless man in black,
What is that donkey's cross upon your back,
As the young girls lift their skirts and cry,
O! listless man in sunshine wearing black!'

It is Spring again, the trout feed,
The young sap stirs and flows like sluggish blood;
More people come to Mass and better dressed:
In the mountain I heard the sighing crack of guns
And the mirror in my hand cracked too
And ran in blood and my hands were blood
Until the burning sun came down and stood
Against my sky at three, in blood.

1955

CATHEDRAL TOWN

I lived in Armagh
In a time of war   the most dreamy
Time of my life   Beyond your walls
    Shape of lost surety
    My future lay

    Looming cathedral
Memory shapes you in the air
On a night when a cutting wind
    Marks the glass
    With bursts of rain

    Tall guardian
Of my childhood in the Ulster
Night   overhanging Patrick's city
    Its huddled roofs
    Fringed with rain

    As the iron bell
Swings out again   each quarter's
Notes dwindling down a shaft
    Of present and past
    To drowning monotone

                after a poem by François Monod, 'Reims'

THE SHELTERED EDGE

SPEECH FOR AN IDEAL IRISH ELECTION

1

Then the visionary lady
Walked like a magician's daughter
Across green acres of Ireland;
The broad bright sword
Of the politician's word
Summoned the applause in every square.

2

The unseen inhabited
A well, a corner of a field;
Houses assumed magic light
From patriots' memory;
Assemblies knelt in awe before
The supernatural in a shaking tree.

3

The light that never was
Enlarged profile, gun and phrase:
Green of the grass worn
On shoulder as catalytic token;
Acrid speech of rifle and gun
Easing neurosis into definite action.

4

The house subsides into stillness,
Buried bombs ignore the spade.
The evening light, suitably grave,
Challenges renewed activity.
The transfigured heroes assume
Grey proportions of statuary.

Now the extraordinary hour of calm
And day of limitation.
The soft grasses stir
Where unfinished dreams
Are buried with the Fianna
In that remote rock cave.

Who today asks for more
— Smoke of battle blown aside —
Than the struggle with casual
Graceless unheroic things,
The greater task of swimming
Against a receding tide?

II

CALEDON CASTLE

That was my first glimpse of opulence;
A line of peacocks deployed upon the lawn
Before a wide-windowed house.
And I was five and clutched a larger hand,
Marvelling how the marvellous birds
Expanded their wild tails like fans.
Under the warm trees, the deer grazed,
Under the walls, the peacocks strayed,
Under the windows, stone fountains played,
In a doomed and formal dance of opulence.

III

SLUM CLEARANCE

Standing at the window, I watch the wild green leaves
Lurch back against the wall, all the branches of the apple tree
Stretch tight before the wind, the rain lash
The evening long against the rubbish dumps,
The half-built flats, the oozing grey cement
Of hasty walls, the white-faced children
Deprived of sun, scurrying with sharp laughter
From point to point of shelter,
And arched over all, the indifferent deadening rain.

IV

INCANTATION IN TIME OF PEACE

At times on this island, at the sheltered edge of Europe,
The last flowering garden of prayer and pretence,
Green enclosure of monks and quiet poetry,
Where the rivers move, without haste, to a restless sea,
And the rain shifts like a woven veil
Over headland and sleeping plain;
At times in this island, dreaming all day
In the sunlight and rain of attained revolutions,
We are afraid, as the hints pile up, of disaster,
Armoured as a dinosaur, rising from the salt flats,
The webbed marshes of history, making the hand tremble,
Hardly knowing why.

At times, we watch the gradual progress of days
In this last casual fortress, separate by sea
And by choice from all men's fears and alarms,
All signs of shattered unity referred
To the benign and exclusive care of the Trinity,
Who today in our hour of need, seem indifferent and far
Over the shuttered and graceful hills,

In a more blessed land, where peace is the air,
And praise grazes in every fresh pasture;
There, our withdrawn ancestors, deserving of rest,
Kneel among dark rocks, in incessant
Contemplative prayer.

At times, we turn in most ordinary weakness and trembling
From the incense rising, the gentle light falling
On damp slum tenement and holy mountain;
From the safety of private quarrels, the candid forgiving,
Turn with hands eager in wishing
To assist all those fearful, exiled, and ailing,
Implicit in out-stretched palms
Pulsing from the woven wrists like doves in flight
This need to be sharing,
And know against this backcloth
Our best longings helpless, as the clouds begin banking
For a more ominous day.

1953

WILD SPORTS OF THE WEST

The landlord's coat is tulip red,
A beacon on the wine-dark moor;
He turns his well-bred foreign devil's face,
While his bailiff trots before.

His furious hooves drum fire from stone,
A beautiful sight when gone;
Contemplation holds the noble horseman
In his high mould of bone.

Not so beautiful the bandy bailiff,
Churlish servant of an alien will:
Behind the hedge a maddened peasant
Poises his shotgun for the kill.

Evening brings the huntsman home,
Blood of pheasants in a bag:
Beside a turfrick the cackling peasant
Cleanses his ancient weapon with a rag.

The fox, evicted from the thicket,
Evades with grace the snuffling hounds:
But a transplanted bailiff, in a feudal paradise,
Patrols for God His private grounds.

POISONED LANDS*

'Four good dogs dead in one night
And a rooster, scaly legs in the air,
Beak in the dust, a terrible sight!'
Behind high weathered walls, his share
Of local lands, the owner skulks
Or leaves in dismal guttering gaps
A trail of broken branches, roots,
Bruised by his mournful rubber boots.

Neighbours sight him as a high hat
Dancing down hedges, a skeletal shape
Night-haloed with whistling bats,
Or silhouetted against cloudy skies,
Coat turned briskly to the nape,
Sou'westered in harsh surmise.

'Children dawdling home from Mass
Chased a bouncing ball and found,
Where he had stood, scorched tufts of grass,
Blighted leaves' — and here the sound
Of rodent gossip sank — 'worse by far,
Dark radiance as though a star
Had disintegrated, a clinging stench
Gutting the substances of earth and air.'

At night, like baleful shadowed eyes,
His windows show the way to cars
Igniting the dark like fireflies.
Gusts of song and broken glass
Prelude wild triumphal feasts
Climaxed by sacrifice of beasts.

Privileged, I met him on an evening walk,
Inveigled him into casual weather-talk.
'I don't like country people' he said, with a grin.
The winter sunlight halved his mottled chin
And behind, a white notice seemed to swing and say:
'If you too licked grass, you'd be dead to-day.'

*A sign seen in the Irish countryside which indicates that poisoned meat
has been laid down to destroy predatory animals.

THE MUMMER SPEAKS

'God save our shadowed lands
Stalked by this night beast of the dead
— Turnip roundness of the skull,
Sockets smouldering in the head —
Will no St. George or Patrick come,
Restore to us our once blessed
And blossoming, now barren home?'

He paused on the threshold,
Clashed his sword of wood,
His swinging lantern on the snow
Threw blood-red circles where he stood;
Herded listeners gaped
Like goslings, as if they understood.

Bold as brass, a battering knight
Came roaring through the door,
Bussed the ladies on his right,
Smashed the devil to the floor.
Justice triumphs on the spot,
With straw, like guts, strewn everywhere:
False Satan struts no more.

Seen in womblike darkness,
Two wearing decades ago;
From which I still recall
Their faces like listening animals,
A stormlamp swinging to and fro,
And from those creaking country rhymes,
That purging lament of bad times.

NURSERY STORY

Children learn the first lesson of fear in the night,
Hearing the clock talk as though to itself,
The lost birds crying under the creak of branches,
The drip-drip of a water-tap, and something moving
That could be alive, like a rat or a mouse,
But inhabits the dark without reason.

Islanded in the night, the young and the sleepless hear
The slight edge of the curtain twitching and shifting
And rubbing the dark, the murmur of walls
When dimensions are hidden, and suddenly fear
This absence of clear light, and the family of objects
That can be touched by a finger:

Golliwog with gross eyes dead in a corner,
Jack-in-the-Box who murdered Jack Horner,
Cinderella betrayed by the giant ogre,
Sinbad-the-Sailor with the great Roc on his back,
Stridently calling, and Tom the Piper's son,
Fleeing in fear from a horrible father.

1953

A WELCOMING PARTY
Wie war das möglich?

That final newsreel of the war:
A welcoming party of almost shades
Met us at the cinema door
Clicking what remained of their heels.

From nests of bodies like hatching eggs
Flickered insectlike hands and legs
And rose an ululation, terrible, shy;
Children conjugating the verb 'to die'.

One clamoured mutely of love
From a mouth like a burnt glove;
Others upheld hands bleak as begging bowls
Claiming the small change of our souls.

Some smiled at us as protectors.
Can these bones live?
Our parochial brand of innocence
Was all we had to give.

To be always at the periphery of incident
Gave my childhood its Irish dimension; drama of unevent:
Yet doves of mercy, as doves of air,
Can falter here as anywhere.

That long dead Sunday in Armagh
I learned one meaning of total war
And went home to my Christian school
To kick a football through the air.

THE QUEST

Under the Cretan earth the animal dwelt
That was more than flesh, fabled as myth.
Beneath sharp rocks he searched and pried
Every sun-sapped rigorous mountainside.

The city had lost interest:
Even his chosen friends.
He finds a clue and disappears
Scarcely knowing what the search intends.

To gather the tenuous golden thread?
He was not deceived by touch
Knowing that fingers can betray,
Love be regarded overmuch.

Not moving to a clear and patterned faith,
Knowing only the need to save his breath
For some moving monster in the dark:
His only hint at truth a labyrinth.

With torch and toughened hands
Well equipped:
Layer after layer of the darkness
He stripped,

And came at last, with harsh surprise,
To where in breathing darkness lay
A lonely monster with almost human terror
In its lilac eyes.

1953

CULTURAL CENTER

ROOM I

The central crucifix from which the rigid figure
Hangs, minatory and Catalan;
The robust contours of an imperial brow,
Nose bridge spanned according to a law,
With lips that barely condescend to form a kiss
(Since Roman virtue is chief end on earth
And desire sufficient without spirit's rebirth);
While in a corner the Indian God
With multiplying hands, makes strange appeal
For concord, even in a place crowded
And wild with views as this:
His is a sort of benign and universal kiss.

ROOM II

Through corridors, in juxtaposed grace
Conflicting modes assume their permanence.
This lady has the high Renaissance face
Of a Botticelli virgin in vernal radiance;
This tapestry has birds that lift their wings
In gestures of freedom from the woven silk.
How lightly the Japanese mountain rests its weight,
As though not intending to offend the earth!
And all this delicacy confronts, affronts,
The stark and staring crucifix.

ROOM III

Europe is dying, these motions say,
With this sharp body twisted all awry,
These diagrams of horror from a burnt-out city,
A canvas sprawling like a battlefield, with slaughtered forms,
While bright and clear, subduing all,
A complete abstraction judges us
From its clean white wall.

ENTRANCE HALL

A tiny nun is leading her whole class
Of chattering girls, through buildings
Perfectly constructed from pure glass,
To where this version of her vision stands:
At her corded waist swings
A minute harmless god of silver plate,
Until at last, inoffensive, starched and mild,
She stands possessively beneath
The lean, accusing, Catalan crucifix.

New Haven, 1954

BUS STOP, NEVADA

The blind, the halt, the lame descend these steps.
This cheapest form of transport gets its trade
From God's worst handiwork, the botched and poorly paid
In a land of honey. The anaemic lady,
The heavy shop-girl rush into desert sunlight,
Blazing a trail with comic books and smoke
To where, in a sullen cafeteria,
Coffee-engines snort and cheap pies line the glass.
Hands ply the glossy cranks of slot-machines,
Dreaming catharsis through a deluge of coins.
Beyond, the snow-capped sierras bluntly rise:
Suggest, even in high summer, skiers' curving ease.
Travellers raise their bored and famished eyes
To where snow and forest rim the endless skies.

1955

CONSTRUCT A CITY

Construct a great city, with music and movement,
Light on the battlements,
Dark rising stairs,
Where the heroes ascend bearing high flaring torches
And an ancient castle's eye
Impassively stares.

Raise a great monument, stone or alabaster,
With heavy solid hands,
And a Buddha's quiescent face
Overlooking the dark sea-winding approaches
Of this fictive city
With a historic grimace.

Here grace and ritual have created a policy,
Moulding life over into stately play:
Only one element lacks to such grave perfection
When frightened sentries sight
Ranked predatory galleys
Move into the bay.

                                        1952

ABOVE THE POOL

We were nearly
pressed against each other
on the stairs
(you, one step above
with your mother:
I, one step below
with my aunt)

of the white mosque
of a cinema
in Bundoran, high above
the small hotels, ice-cream
parlours, the Atlantic
working against
Roguey rocks.

And my eyes
were asking yours,
and yours were asking mine
for something more
than a glance on a stair;
the seawrack odour
of Donegal air.

We crossed
on the wooden stairs
above the bathing pool
next day, and you halted
with your sun-warmed hair
expectant eyes, wedge-heeled
wartime shoes

waiting for me
to speak, while hit tunes
from the Majestic ballroom
sobbed in my brain:
*I'll close my eyes,
Shine on, Victory Moon,*

And I walked on
balancing all my hunger for
that mysterious other
against my need to be alone,
to hug rocks, search blue pools
for starfish, in this
my last summer of loneliness.

SIRENS

The crazy hooting of sirens
Fills my sleep with news of loss:
By the quays the shadowy ships
In darkness toss on untidy waters,
Gathering silence around their bows
And a fitful midmonth moon
Moves across dark roofs,
Carelessly bestowing light.

Inland, across projected lands of grief,
The ominous birds of night
Make the sky their passage-way
To chanting, clanging rookery:
And swaying heads of trees rehearse
With pluck and toss, ritual of dalliance,
Heart's blind need, at time of loss,
To be like bird or boat, departing someplace.

1952

SONG OF THE LONELY BACHELOR

They at least possess a secret, moving hands
As though each touch were Midas, making gold:
They at least possess a way and motion
That stills disturbance, if only a shared panacea
Against the pain of growing old.

At least. The sensual being often
Close as the coupled get to good;
The shared possessions, the talks at table,
The renewal after quarrels, a way of living
Not entirely rude.

Within this magic circle of young lovers
The intruder hesitantly moves;
Leans nearer only to discover
In that velvet purring silence
The noisy rubbing of his shoes.

1952

WEDDING SONG

Willow and lilac by the water's edge
Reach into the river;
A young girl strides down
To the water's edge,
Turning a ring on her finger.
All the phenomena of summer
Tend, attend her,
Subject to her beckoning finger.

Willow, lilac,
Reign green and gold forever,
Shape her young figure
Within a flowering border
Like a Victorian picture,
Antique and clear:
Let the water-lilies clash
Slight swords in the air.

A young girl walked under
Lilac and willow
To the water's edge
Of a mid-western river.
From far off I send
My wishes to follow her,
Once glimpsed, once loved
By a bright summer water.

PASTORALS

I

'Lyricize this, my fretful love,
Love is a claw within a velvet glove,
Love is a movement of a withered hand,
Love is a dawn illusion
Blandly planned:
How can brief blood understand?'

II

'Love is the movement of the race
Blood-blindfolded to a chosen face:
Movement of unlawful limbs
In a marriage of two whims:
Consummation of disgrace
Beneath the burning-glass of grace.'

III

And yet, my love, we two have come
Into love as to a lighted room
Where all is gaiety and humbling grace.
Hearts long bruised with indolence,
With harsh fatigue of unrelated fact, can trace
Redeeming patterns of experience.

IRISH STREET SCENE, WITH LOVERS

A rainy quiet evening, with leaves that hang
Like squares of silk from dripping branches.
An avenue of laurel, and the guttering cry
Of a robin that balances a moment,
Starts and is gone
Upon some furtive errand of its own.

A quiet evening, with skies washed and grey;
A tiredness as though the day
Swayed towards sleep,
Except for the reserved statement
Of rain on the stone-grey pavement —
Dripping, they move through this marine light,

Seeming to swim more than walk,
Linked under the black arch of an umbrella,
With its assembly of spokes like points of stars,
A globule of water slowly forming on each.
The world shrinks to the soaked, worn
Shield of cloth they parade beneath.

1952

BY THE FOUNTAIN, STEPHEN'S GREEN, DUBLIN

Dream, child, by the nullity of the water.
A gull curls up its quaint scaled toes
And jabs wedged wings at the sky.
Women at their knitting die in their chairs.
Your world now moves in wool and purl
And calmness settling as milk in a glass,
Frothing and cool. O! where come warnings
Into this isolated patch
With its limited radiances of green and quiet?
Calmness is a day, folded comfortably, neatly
Over the knees, like a rug on a chair;
Nothing demanded but planned, peaceful posture,
Thoughts frozen in clean air.

1950

WOODTOWN MANOR

for Morris Graves

I

Here the delicate dance of silence,
The quick step of the robin,
The sudden skittering rush of the wren:
Minute essences move in and out of creation
Until the skin of soundlessness forms again.

Part order, part wilderness,
Water creates its cadenced illusion
Of glaucous, fluent growth;
Fins raised, as in a waking dream,
Bright fish probe their painted stream.

Imaginary animals harbour here:
The young fox coiled in its covert,
Bright-eyed and mean, the baby bird:
The heron, like a tilted italic,
Illuminating the gospel of the absurd.

And all the menagerie of the living marvellous:
Stone shape of toad,
Flicker of insect life,
Shift of wind touched grass
As though a beneficent spirit stirred.

II

Twin deities hover in Irish air
Reconciling poles of east and west;
The detached and sensual Indian God,
Franciscan dream of gentleness:
Gravity of Georgian manor
Approves, with classic stare,
Their dual disciplines of tenderness.

CHINESE POETRY

For the long summer evenings; boating,
The river cool and imperceptibly sliding,
The boats disturbing the water-lilies,
Lying yellow and heavy on the face of the water,
Like dripping pats of butter on a patterned plate.

For the long nights; a mild wind between tenuous trees,
A seat with friends on the shaded terrace,
Rejoicing in the sun's heat, stored in body and timber,
And drinking the twilight easily away, until the moon
Sings to herself, in a blue emptiness of sky.

For the cool mornings; late rising in a sunlit room,
And then strolling alone in the Apricot Gardens,
Where a world goes walking, boasting and scheming;
Or more pleasantly still, like many ladies, goes riding,
Held lightly aloft on the shoulders of others.

The poet, however, does not meditate schemes of action,
Or look in every face for a beloved, but thinks of his friends,
And of his last lyrics, insignificant but difficult things.

1952

KENMARE BAY

for Michael Scott

Caha to the south, MacGillicuddy to the north,
This bay lies, a giant bowl
Of blue water, held reverently
Between enormous palms.

Villages in valleys
Semaphore their presence
With a glitter of windows
From a far tilled coast,

Where fields clamber the mountains
Laboriously as persons,
To falter into granite,
Underbelly of cloud.

A frieze of pines
Provides green peace for a black crow
To holler at the sea
And at the motor-boat

Which noses between
Seaweeded islands, rhinestone inlets,
Scattering the sea-pies
Whose red beaks flash

Above visitors' hats
Like scalping knives.

TRAPPER

To keep his family alive during the war years
He trapped rabbits. The gold coil of a snare
Caught at one's foot in meadow grass
Or the cry of a rabbit, as he passed
On his rounds in the morning.

Daily a dozen rabbits died, to provide his income.
He would break the animal's neck
With a sideways crack of his hand.
Strung up in our barn, they ran their last
Race towards earth's centre, mossy teeth bared.

And yet there always seemed to be more rabbits.
There was a hill, honeycombed with burrows
Where they sat at twilight. You could hear
A hazel nut fall in the silence
Before, suddenly, they were out of sight,

Only pellets of dung to recall their presence.

1959

TIM

Not those slim-flanked fillies
slender-ankled as models
glimpsed across the rails
through sunlong afternoons
as with fluent fetlocks
they devoured the miles

Nor at some Spring Show
a concourse of Clydesdales
waiting, huge as mammoths,
as enormous hirsute dolls,
for an incongruous rose to
blossom behind their ears

Nor that legendary Pegasus
leaping towards heaven:
only those hold my affection
who, stolid as weights,
rested in the rushy
meadows of my childhood

Or rumbled down lanes,
lumbering before carts.
Tim, the first horse I rode,
seasick on his barrel
back; the first to lip
bread from my hand.

I saw the end of your road.
You stood, with gouged eyeball
while our farmhand swabbed
the hurt socket out with
water and Jeyes Fluid:
as warm an object of

loving memory, as any
who have followed me
to this day, denying
rhetoric with your patience,
forcing me to drink
from the trough of reality.

1960 -'76

THE LAST MONSTER

First, the dodo disappeared,
Leaving a legend of a simpleton's head,
Grotesque nut-cracker nose:
But a rum, a rare old one,
With feathers like old clothes.

The great Auk struck out for St. Kilda's,
Settled with shaggy Highlanders,
Skin divers and such:
Learned the language of oblivion,
Finally lost touch.

Gone also, as Goldsmith noted,
The bird of Nazareth and the lesser tatou,
Beasts of strange pattern and birds past belief:
Even to number their names, like witchcraft,
Affords sensual relief.

Golden-pawed snowman of Everest,
Wildcat of the Grampians,
Bower-bird of Peru:
Stay hidden wherever you are,
The final inventory is after you!

Somewhere on the ultimate scarp
The last monster will watch
With hooded eyes,
While tiny men trek importantly towards him,
Bristling with strange supplies.

PORTRAIT OF THE ARTIST
AS A MODEL FARMER

Wild provincials
Muttering into microphones
Declare that art
Springs only from the native part;
That like a potato it best grows
Planted deep in local rows:

Local loam and local air,
Local sods and horse manure,
Watered by a local rain,
Good for the vegetable brain.
This potato I plant deep
In my candid garden heap

And like a sympathetic farmer
Shield from all might harm her,
Foreign beetles and exotic weeds,
Complicated continental breeds:
And when my baby tuber
To its might has grown

I shall come into my provincial own
And mutter deep
In my living sleep
Of the tradition that I keep.
My tiny spud will comfort me
In my fierce anonymity.

THE FIRST INVASION OF IRELAND

for Michael Walsh

According to Leabhar Gabhála, *The Book of Conquests, the first invasion of Ireland was by relatives of Noah, just before the Flood. Refused entry into the Ark, they consulted an idol which told them to flee to Ireland. There were three men and fifty-one women in the party and their behaviour has so little in common with subsequent tradition in Ireland that one must take the story to be mythological.*

Fleeing from threatened flood, they sailed,
Seeking the fair island, without serpent or claw;
From the deck of their hasty raft watched
The soft edge of Ireland nearward draw.

A sweet confluence of waters, a trinity of rivers,
Was their first resting place:
They unloaded the women and the sensual idol,
Guiding image of their disgrace.

Division of damsels they did there,
The slender, the tender, the dimpled, the round,
It was the first just bargain in Ireland,
There was enough to go round.

Lightly they lay and pleasured
In the green grass of that guileless place:
Ladhra was the first to die;
He perished of an embrace.

Bith was buried in a stone heap,
Riot of mind, all passion spent.
Fintan fled from the ferocious women
Lest he, too, by love be rent.

Great primitive princes of our line —
They were the first, with stately freedom,
To sleep with women in Ireland:
Soft the eternal bed they lie upon.

On a lonely headland the women assembled,
Chill as worshippers in a nave,
And watched the eastern waters gather
Into a great virile flooding wave.

WALKING THE DOG

Recovering from an illness
I walk a neighbour's dog
Each day in the Champ de Mars:
A sleek Cocker spaniel
With long golden ears —
Thirty quid's worth of silky hair.

With a visage grave as Richelieu
Contemplating the state of France
He examines his universe
Of smells and excrement:
Every puddle provokes
A sensual trance.

Across two lawns
He sights a friend
Possible for love
And gallops to attend:
The excitement is intense —
Inspection at either end.

He circulates a bench
To distribute his signature
Adapting to double purpose
This rank poetry of the poor:
Generations to come
Will know his noble spoor.

Pulled from pillar to post
By this most pampered beast
I certainly ought to protest —
Enough's as good as a feast —
But follow in baffled awe
Shameless manhood, golden fleece.

STORM

I watch the rain
beat on the gray road;
drops pelt and leap,
sharp as fish hooks.

A man leans slowly
into his bicycle,
yellow cape flapping;
a bedraggled butterfly.

Another tramps past,
a sack on his head,
herding the cattle inside,
broad hides steaming.

As the thunder groans
and breaks we kneel
in a circle to intone
a decade of the Rosary.

Lightning joins that room
to the one I now stare from;
the child to the grown man:
art, a warm brooding.

1960-'76

VISIT

for Robert Graves

In a master's presence
One should incline the head,
Not parry or question.
Though it terrifies
You now, with luck
You too may harden
Into the rough rocksalt
Of such opinion.

P6